Zeke and the Big Sand Cake

Jill McDougall

Illustrated by Tom Bonson

Zeke was at Space School.

“It’s play time,” said Mr Moon.

Everyone ran outside.

Zeke ran to the sand pit.

"I will make a big cake," he said.

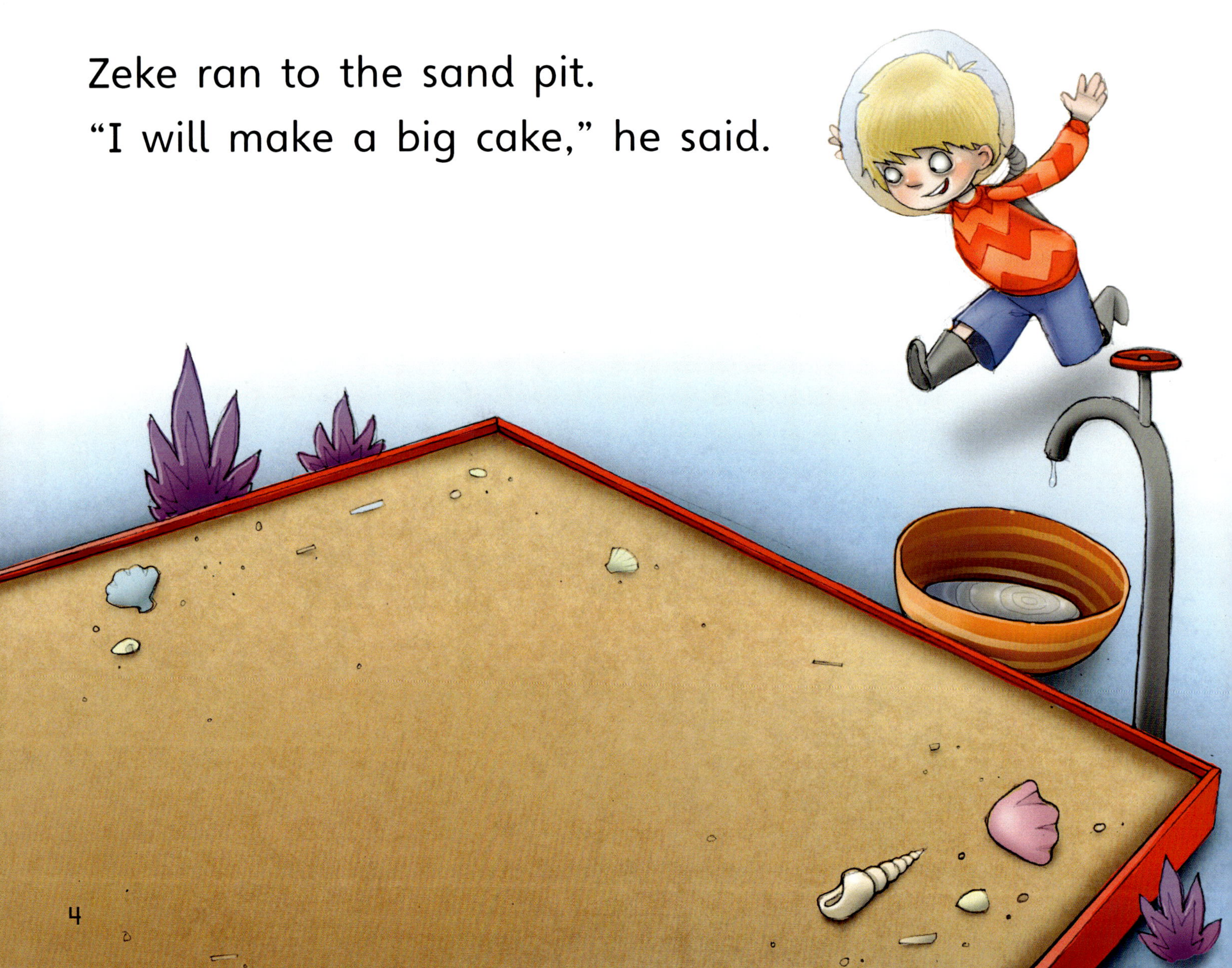

Zeke put some wet sand in a bucket.
He patted the sand and tipped it out.
“My cake looks good,” said Zeke. “But it is too small.”

Zeke's friend Blip came over.
"I will help you make a big cake," said Blip.
Blip put more sand on the cake.

Oh no! The cake went flat.

“I can fix the cake,” said Zeke.
Zeke got some more sand.
The cake grew bigger and **bigger**!

“Here are some shells,” said Blip.
“They will look good on the cake.”
Oh no! Blip put his foot in the cake.

“I can fix it,” said Zeke.

He put some more sand on the cake.

The cake grew bigger and **bigger**…

and **bigger!**

Mr Moon came to look.
"I will take a photo," he said.

“Wait!” said Blip.
“I have a flower for the cake.”
He came running.

Oh no! Blip fell over.

He fell on top of the cake!

“Ha! Ha!” said Zeke.

“Now we have a big, flat *pancake*!”